Idioms for IELTS Speaking:

Master IELTS Vocabulary to Get a Higher Band Score

www.eslspeaking.org

Jackie Bolen

Table of Contents

4

5

Introduction

Welcome to this book designed to help you expand your knowledge of idioms, expressions and phrases in American English. My goal is to help you expand your vocabulary and to be able to speak and write more fluently.

Let's face it, idioms can be difficult to master, even for the best students. In this book, you'll find hundreds of English idioms and phrases that are used in boardrooms, over a meal, and with friends and family around the world.

The best way to learn new vocabulary is in context. That's why each idiom comes with some example sentences. You'll also find a simple explanation in plain English for each one as well as the origin of the idiom if it's known.

To get the most bang for your buck, be sure to do the following:

- Review frequently.

- Use each idiom or phrase in real life as soon as possible.

- Don't be nervous about making mistakes. That's how you'll get better at English!

- Consider studying with a friend to help each other stay motivated.

Good luck and I wish you well on your journey to becoming more proficient with idioms in American English.

About the Author: Jackie Bolen

I taught English in South Korea for 10 years to every level and type of student. I've taught every age from kindergarten kids to adults. Most of my time has centered around teaching at two universities: five years at a science and engineering school in Cheonan, and four years at a major university in Busan where I taught upper-level classes for students majoring in English. In my spare time, you can usually find me outside surfing, biking, hiking, or snowshoeing. I now live in Vancouver, Canada.

In case you were wondering what my academic qualifications are, I hold a Master of Arts in Psychology. During my time in Korea, I completed both the Cambridge CELTA and DELTA certification programs. With the combination of almost ten years teaching ESL/EFL learners of all ages and levels, and the more formal teaching qualifications I've obtained, I have a solid foundation on which to offer advice to English learners.

I truly hope that you find this book useful. I would love it if you sent me an email with any questions or feedback that you might have.

Jackie Bolen (www.jackiebolen.com)

Twitter: @bolen_jackie

Email: jb.business.online@gmail.com

You might also be interested in this book: Advanced English Conversation Dialogues (by Jackie Bolen). You can easily find it wherever you like to buy books It has hundreds of helpful English phrases and expressions that can be used in a wide variety of situations. Learn to speak more fluently in American English.

An Introduction to the IELTS Speaking Test

The IELTS speaking test is the same, whether you choose the general or academic version of the test. It's face-to-face with a real person, as opposed to some other English proficiency tests where you speak into a voice recorder. However, each IELTS speaking test is recorded to ensure quality control.

The test takes 11-14 minutes and consists of 3 parts:

1. **Part 1:** The first set consists of general questions about where you work, study or live. There will be two other question sets after that on personal topics such as clothing, holidays, food, etc. It takes 4-5 minutes and will consist of approximately 12 questions in total.

2. **Part 2:** Speaking for 1-2 minutes about a topic that will be given to you. You will have 1 minute of preparation time. There may be one short follow-up question.

3. **Part 3:** A 4-5 minute discussion that goes into greater depth about the topic from part 2. The examiner has freedom to ask follow-up questions based on your answers. The discussion will be about general ideas and not personal ones (like in part 1). Think of this section as more of a 2-way dialogue with the examiner.

The speaking and listening portions of the test are the same, whether you choose the general or academic version of it. It's the reading and writing portions that are different. Be sure to check closely which test is required for whatever purpose you're taking the test for. The general test is usually required for immigration purposes while the academic one is most often required for college entrance.

How is the IELTS Speaking Test Graded?

You will be graded on four things:

1. **Fluency and coherence:** How quickly you speak, without pauses or repeating yourself. Is the previous thought connected to the next one and how do you finish off what you're saying?

2. **Lexical resources (vocabulary):** To score at the band 7 level, or above, you'll need to be able to speak about all the topics on the test with precision, as well as use things like collocations (words that occur together more often than by random chance), idioms, slang, and phrasal verbs. This book will focus on helping you with this!

3. **Grammatical range and accuracy:** To score at the highest levels, you'll need to be able to form a variety of simple and complex sentences accurately. The keys are to use a variety of sentence types and to make few errors.

4. **Pronunciation:** You'll need to be able to be understood very easily, without any effort on the part of the examiner. Plus, you'll have to put emphasize on the correct words within a sentence and also within a longer speaking turn.

Tips for Getting a Higher Score on IELTS Speaking

For most proficient English speakers, getting a band 7 or 8 on the IELTS speaking test is a very achievable goal. Here are a few tips for getting there!

- One of the keys is striking a balance between giving enough detail in your answers to develop topics fully and not talking too much. The examiner has a prescribed set of questions that they need to get through within a strict time limit. Pause when you're done with your thought. The examiner will ask another question.

- Don't feel the need to keep talking, and talking, and talking, and talking. This is not how this test works and you will not get a higher score just because you are able to talk endlessly. This can hurt you if you begin to repeat yourself.

- Don't repeat yourself but do connect the things you say in an organized way with the use of discourse markers: as I previously mentioned, firstly, after that, finally, etc.

- Being able to paraphrase and summarize things is quite important for the test. Aim for a balance between giving some details and also giving a summary or overview of things.

- Do NOT attempt to memorize anything for this test. You will get penalized very heavily for this and it is a waste of time. There are so many questions each year that even if you were to find out some of them, it's impossible to memorize that many answers.

- Use idioms, phrasal verbs, slang (appropriate!), collocations, etc. Not using idiomatic language will make it difficult to score above a Band 6.

- Aim to use precise words to describe something, instead of words like "thing, stuff, like that." This shows that you don't have a large vocabulary, or can't access it when needed. Avoid filler words that don't have any meaning.

- It's easy to repeat words as a kind of filler (the author of this book says, "like" way too much!) when speaking. However, this should be avoided. Look on Google for some sample IELTS speaking test questions and then record yourself answering them to see if there are words that you use too often. Like is the most common one of these kinds of words but there are lots more.

- Use a mix of complex and simple sentences. Even if you use simple sentences perfectly, it will make it difficult to score above a Band 5.

- Finish off your thoughts in an appropriate way. Ending most sentences with: like that, that's why, that's it, or something similar will make it difficult to score above a band 6.

- Show your personality. Emphasize key things in what you're saying and don't be scared to show your opinion about something. The examiner is only grading you on your English ability, not on your opinions about a topic.

- Using humour or telling a (short!) funny story about something is great. It's a nice way to show that you know English quite well if you're able to do this.

- For part 3, don't get personal. This section is designed to test your ability to talk about general ideas and thoughts which is more difficult to do than talking about personal things. This is the section where candidates can set themselves apart and have a chance to use higher-level vocabulary and grammatical constructions.

How Difficult is it to Score Band 9?

It's quite difficult (though not impossible) for non-native English speakers to achieve a band 9 on the IELTS speaking test. There are people who have been learning English as a second language (most Europeans for example) since they were a young child and they also have a first language that is similar to English. For these people, it may be achievable.

Or, there are some people who moved to an English speaking country when they were young who may be able to get this score. Or, those who did a large part of their education in English.

However, being a native English speaker doesn't automatically mean that you'll be able to get a 9. It's not that easy to do! To do that, you'll also need to do the following:

- Develop topics fully and at length.

- Connect thoughts, without repetition.

- Only have pauses that are related to forming an opinion about something, for example and not searching for a word (no pauses in the middle of sentences).

- Use a large range of very precise language, including things like idioms.

- Speak fluently, essentially without grammatical errors.

- Be understood easily, without any effort on the part of the examiner.

- Avoid the use of filler words (this is what even native speakers may struggle with).

The good news is that there is almost no reason why someone would need to get a 9 on this test. For educational, immigration, employment or other purposes, I don't know of any of them that would require getting a 9! So, don't worry about it. Scoring a 7 or 8 on the speaking test is a far more achievable goal and should be acceptable in almost all cases.

A bee in my bonnet

Meaning: A certain, specific issue that is annoying someone.

Origin: First seen in the 1500s. Came from the Scottish idiom, "A head full of bees." It's evident how annoying a bee buzzing around in your hat (bonnet) would be.

Example IELTS question: Describe a time when two of your friends or family members had a conflict.

Possible answer: Well, my sister and my dad are always fighting. My sister is messy and my dad has *a bee in his bonnet* about the house always being organized. It leads to a lot of conflict between them.

Add insult to Injury

Meaning: Make something already bad worse. For example, a guy fell off his bike but then a car ran over his foot.

Origin: Possibly from the ancient Roman fable of a bald man and a fly. The man tried to crush a fly on his head but used too much force and hurt himself too.

Example IELTS question: Do you like your job?

Possible answer: It pays well but there are some negatives. For example, I often have to work overtime on the weekends. *To add insult to injury*, it's usually not paid.

A dime a dozen

Meaning: Something that is very common; not special.

Origin: First seen in the early 1800s when you could often buy a dozen (12) things for $0.10 (a dime).

Example IELTS question: Is marketing a popular job in your country?

Possible answer: Yes, for sure. Marketing and PR people are *a dime a dozen* in all of Europe. It can be quite difficult for them to get jobs unless they have some sort of specialized skill like paid advertising.

A hard nut to crack (A tough nut to crack)

Meaning: Someone who is difficult to get to know.

Origin: Used since the 1700s. Refers to how it's not easy to open a nut because of the hard shell. Depending on the nut, it's not possible to do it without a special tool.

Example IELTS question: Can you describe your best friend?

Possible answer: Sure, her name is Cindy and we've known each other for 10 years now. She's *a tough nut to crack* when you first meet her, but after a while, she warms up and is very generous and loyal.

Ahead of the pack

Meaning: To be ahead of other people or companies trying to do a similar thing.

Origin: "Pack" has been used to refer to a group of people since the 1400s. Or, it could be a reference to pack animals like dogs that have a leader that goes near the front.

Example IELTS question: What's your favourite website?

Possible answer: I often check out techcrunch.com. I love to be *ahead of the pack* when it comes to technology and I usually have the latest gadget. It can be quite an expensive hobby though!

A lot on my plate

Meaning: Many responsibilities.

Origin: First used in the 1900s. Refers to a plate that's heaping full of food and difficult to balance when carrying it to a table. Now, imagine those are your responsibilities!

Example IELTS question: What do you usually do in the evenings?

Possible answer: Well, I have *a lot on my plate* with two young children at home so evenings are usually spent making dinner, cleaning up, doing laundry and putting them to bed. All the chores that need to get done in a busy household. After that stuff is done, I'm usually tired so I just watch some Netflix for a couple of hours.

An apple a day keeps the doctor away

Meaning: Eating healthy keeps you from getting sick.

Origin: First seen in the late 1800s to early 1900s in Wales. In old English, an apple could refer to any round fruit so it may be related to the fact that healthy eating is vital for good health.

Example IELTS question: Do you have a healthy diet?

Possible answer: In general, I think I eat a reasonably healthy diet. My mom always used to say something similar to, "*An apple a day keeps the doctor away*." As I've gotten older, I've started to see how true that is!

A piece of cake

Meaning: Something that's easy to do.

Origin: From the 1870s. Cakes were often given as prizes during competitions and at fairs so that's why they're associated with something being easy to do.

Example IELTS question: Why did you choose your field of study?

Possible answer: Honestly, I'm a little bit of a lazy student and my friend told me that this course was *a piece of cake* but would lead to a well-paying job. It's not as easy as she said but it's still not that difficult and most people get jobs quite easily after they graduate.

As far as I can tell

Meaning: To the best of my understanding.

Origin: Unknown.

Example IELTS question: Do you think people in your country are generally happy?

Possible answer: As far as I can tell, maybe not! In Korea, people work extremely long hours and have very little time for leisure or just hanging out and relaxing. And students have to study a lot more than here in Canada.

As fit as a fiddle

Meaning: In great shape.

Origin: From England in the 1600s. Initially used to mean well-suited but "fit" later came to be known as in good shape. A fiddle is used because of the alliteration (fit/fiddle) and also because it's a nicely shaped instrument.

Example IELTS question: Tell me about an older person that you admire.

Possible answer: I admire my grandfather. He's 90 years old now but is still *fit as a fiddle*. He plays tennis and can sometimes even beat me! Plus, he never eats junk food. I'm sure he'll live to be 100.

A storm is brewing

Meaning: Difficulty or danger is expected in the future.

Origin: Unknown but could be related to sailors reading the signs in the ocean and sky to predict a coming storm.

Example IELTS question: Describe a journey that didn't go as planned.

Possible answer: I'd like to talk about my brother and I going to Argentina. He was so disorganized and hadn't packed a thing even the night before. I could tell that *a storm was brewing* and that he'd for sure forget something important. As it turned out, he forgot his passport which caused us to miss our flight because we had to go back home to get it.

A tough pill to swallow (A bitter pill to swallow)

Meaning: Something difficult to get over or accept.

Origin: First seen in the 1600s. Probably related to medicine pills that can be big or bitter when you have to swallow them.

Example IELTS question: Describe an unexpected event.

Possible answer: I remember when I took the road test for my driver's license the first time and I failed. I was very confident in my abilities so it was *a tough pill to swallow*. But, looking back on it, the examiner was correct in that I wasn't a safe driver at that time!

At the eleventh hour

Meaning: At the last minute.

Origin: Possibly from Mathew 20:9 in the Bible. In this story, each worker received a denarius (unit of currency) for a day of work, even those who started at hour 11 in a 12-hour day.

Example IELTS question: Describe a zoo or aquarium near your home.

Possible answer: I live right by the Vancouver aquarium and have been there a couple of times. During Covid, it didn't have any revenue coming in and was maybe going to have to shut down. However, they got enough donations *at the eleventh hour* that they were able to remain open.

Bang for the buck

Meaning: Something that offers good value for the money you paid for it.

Origin: Bang = excitement and buck = money. Could be a play on Pepsi's advertising campaign from the 1950s, "More bounce to the ounce."

Example IELTS question: What's one of your favourite restaurants?

Possible answer: Oh, I love Pho Love. It's a Vietnamese place with soup and Ban Mi, a kind of sandwich. Whatever you order, you get a lot of *bang for the buck* as the portions are huge and if you take it home, you have enough for another meal the next day.

Barking up the wrong tree

Meaning: Blaming the wrong person.

Origin: From the 1800s in the USA where hunting dogs would bark at the base of a tree when they thought a wild animal like a raccoon was in it so that their owners could shoot it. But, the wild animal had sometimes already escaped which left the dogs barking at the wrong tree.

Example IELTS question: Do you like your neighbors?

Possible answer: I get along well with most of my neighbors. However, one of them always blames me for leaving dog poop on his lawn. He's *barking up the wrong tree* though—I'm careful to always pick it up.

Beat around the bush

Meaning: Avoid talking about something important, or not getting to the main point directly.

Origin: From the early 1400s. Rich men used to hire people to beat the bushes when they went hunting to scare the birds out of them so that they could shoot them.

Example IELTS question: Do you get along well with your colleagues at work?

Possible answer: Generally yes, except for one of them. She is famous for *beating around the bush* and talking way too much at meetings. I think she just likes hearing her own voice!

Beat me to the punch

Meaning: Say or do something before someone else.

Origin: From the early 1900s with reference to boxing. Sometimes, it's possible to win with just one punch by knocking someone out before they even hit you.

Example IELTS question: Do you usually have the same routine every day?

Possible answer: I generally have the same routine on weekdays. However, my wife sometimes gets up earlier than usual and *beats me to the punch* for getting in the shower. In that case, I'll have breakfast first and then shower afterwards.

Behind the scenes

Meaning: What happens out of sight from the public.

Origin: Refers to backstage at a performance of some kind. It's what the audience can't see.

Example IELTS question: What do you think of fast food?

Possible answer: Well, at face value, it's quite cheap, tastes good and is convenient. However, there's a lot going on *behind the scenes* with regards to animal cruelty and low wages for employees so I generally try to avoid it.

Bend over backwards

Meaning: Work extra hard; go out of your way to do something special for someone.

Origin: From the 900s. Refers to a gymnast bending his back which is not that easy to do unless you're very flexible.

Example IELTS question: Do you like your job?

Possible answer: My job isn't bad. I get paid quite a good wage and there's only one main downside—I *bend over backwards* for them but they don't appreciate it.

Better late than never

Meaning: Encouragement after getting a late start to something.

Origin: First seen in 1396 in the *Canterbury Tales*.

Example IELTS question: How has teaching changed in your country in the past few decades?

Possible answer: One big change is that corporal punishment is now banned. It should have happened a long time ago, but *better late than never* I guess.

Bite the bullet

Meaning: Resolve to do something difficult.

Origin: Unknown. But, one theory is that patients had to bite a bullet when undergoing surgery before anesthesia was developed to endure the pain. However, a leather strap was most often used for this purpose and not a bullet.

Example IELTS question: Do you like shopping?

Possible answer: My problem is that I like shopping too much and spend so much money on it! My husband gets quite angry when I go on a shopping spree so I had to *bite the bullet* and give him all my credit cards.

Blessing in disguise

Meaning: Something that initially seems bad which turns out good in the end. For example, someone lost their job but ended up getting a better job three months later.

Origin: First seen in the 1700s but the origin is unknown.

Example IELTS question: Do people in your country enjoy eating out?

Possible answer: Well, before Covid people used to eat out all the time. Then, dining in restaurants shut down for almost two years which turned out to be a *blessing in disguise*. People started getting back to basics and cooking healthier food at home.

Blow off some steam

Meaning: Doing something to get rid of stress. For example, venting loudly about something frustrating.

Origin: Comes from the early days of railroads. Trains had no safety valves then so engineers would have to release or blow off some steam to prevent an explosion.

Example IELTS question: How do you relax?

Possible answer: I love to go to the gym after work and *blow off some steam*. My job is quite stressful so running on the treadmill or lifting weights is a nice way to chill out.

Born with a silver spoon in his mouth

Meaning: Someone who comes from a wealthy family who doesn't have to work that hard in life.

Origin: It likely began in the middle ages when people would bring their own spoons to the table when they ate. A silver spoon as opposed to a wood one was an indicator of wealth.

Example IELTS question: Describe a person you know who is kind.

Possible answer: One of my cousins is very kind. Although she was *born with a silver spoon in her mouth*, she never acts like it. She's constantly volunteering for different charities and donates much of her salary each year.

Break the bank

Meaning: Something that costs a lot or more than you can afford.

Origin: From the 1600s. Referred to gamblers winning more than the house (referred to as a bank) could afford.

Example IELTS question: How can the government help unemployed people?

Possible answer: I think there could be way more training programs for unemployed people.

It wouldn't *break the bank* and it would benefit employers to have more highly skilled workers, particularly in the trades or technical areas.

Break out in a cold sweat

Meaning: To be afraid or nervous about something.
Origin: Unknown but first seen around the 1500s. When some people get nervous, they sweat but also feel cold.
Example IELTS question: What do you usually do in the evenings?

Possible answer: Well, these days I'm trying to get my driver's license so I'm practicing with my friend. I'm terrified of driving and *break out into a cold sweat* when I even think about taking the road test. But I should be able to do it within the next couple of months I think.

Bring a lot to the table

Meaning: Have a lot of skills, money, wisdom, talent, etc.
Origin: Could refer to the amount of money that a gambler brings to the table to play with. Or, social or religious feasts where everyone is expected to contribute something to the table.
Example IELTS question: Do you get along with your manager at work?

Possible answer: Yes, definitely. I have a lot of respect for her and she's always treated me fairly. She *brings a lot to the table* as well—she's been working in real estate for more than 30 years now.

Bring home the bacon

Meaning: Make money with a job.
Origin: Likely popular with the African-American community in the USA before this but first seen in print in 1908. In 1906 Joe Gans' mother sent him a telegram telling him to "bring

home the bacon" before his lightweight championship boxing match.

Example IELTS question: If you had the chance, would you change your job in the future?

Possible answer: 100%, yes! I don't like working in a factory but someone has to *bring home the bacon* in my family. If I could, I'd probably go back to school and do something like a business degree so that I could get an office job.

Burning the midnight oil

Meaning: Working very long hours, late into the night.

Origin: First seen in the 1600s. Candles and oil were used to provide light before electricity so refers to someone working late into the night.

Example IELTS question: How much do you work?

Possible answer: I work way too much, particularly around year-end. Accountants have to *burn the midnight oil* pretty much all of February and March.

Burn the candle at both ends

Meaning: Work very hard from early morning to late at night.

Origin: The early meaning of this idiom was to be frugal. Candles were expensive so if you wanted to save money, you'd burn both ends. Later, it was used to refer to working too hard, possibly burning the first end of the candle but wanting to continue work so burning the other end too.

Example IELTS question: Do you like your subject at college?

Possible answer: Yes, it's not bad but there are a lot of group projects that take up so much time. Combined with my part-time job, I find that I'm *burning the candle at both ends* most weeks.

Bury my head in the sand

Meaning: To avoid a certain situation or problem.

Origin: Possibly related to ostriches who some observe to hide their heads in bushes when faced with predators. However, this isn't what they do!

Example IELTS question: What can be done to alleviate poverty?

Possible answer: There's a lot that can be done but it's easier for politicians to *bury their heads in the sand* than to deal with it. . .

Busy as a beaver (Busy as a bee)

Meaning: Working a lot or very hard.

Origin: Beavers are very hard workers who spend lots of time building dams and lodges. Same with bees who work very hard to make honey and build hives.

Example IELTS question: How did you celebrate this past holiday?

Possible answer: Christmas is a big holiday in my family. My husband is a serious Christmas enthusiast and he's *as busy as a beaver* getting everything decorated, wrapping presents and making Christmas baking.

Butterflies in my stomach

Meaning: Nervous feeling about something.

Origin: Unknown but seen as early as 1908.

Example IELTS question: Do you often watch sports on TV?

Possible answer: Yes, I'm a huge fan of the Seattle Seahawks and never miss a game. I get *butterflies in my stomach* on game day.

Buttering me up

Meaning: To flatter or please someone because you want something in return. For example, a child who is extra nice to his parents around Christmas because he wants an expensive video game system.

Origin: Possibly from ancient India where people used to throw balls of butter at statues of gods when asking them for favours.

Example IELTS question: What do you usually do on weekends?

Possible answer: On the weekends, I usually spent time doing whatever my kids want! They *butter me up* all week to take them somewhere fun like an amusement park or the lake but I don't mind.

By the book

Meaning: Completely legal, doing something the correct way.

Origin: It's generally thought that the "book" refers to the Bible.

Example IELTS question: Did you enjoy your childhood?

Possible answer: There were some positive and negatives for sure. I got along well with my brother but my dad was very *by the book*. It was okay when I was younger but we had a lot of conflict when I was in my teens because of it.

By the skin of his teeth

Meaning: Just barely succeeding, finishing, etc.

Origin: From Job 19:20 in the Bible: "I am nothing but skin and bones; I have escaped only by the skin of my teeth."

Example IELTS question: Describe a book you recently read.

Possible answer: I read _____. It was about this guy who went hiking and got lost. He only survived *by the skin of his teeth*.

Call it a day

Meaning: To stop working for the rest of the day.

Origin: First recorded use was in 1919 to refer to the end of a workday.

Example IELTS question: How can someone be a better employee?

Possible answer: One thing that most people could do, no matter the job, is to take a look around before they *call it a day* and make sure that they've tied up all the loose ends. I like to use the last 15 minutes of my day to make sure everything is ready for me to start work the following day.

Calm before the storm

Meaning: A quiet period before a difficult period.

Origin: Used by sailors to explain the eerily calm period before a big storm.

Example IELTS question: What is the main environmental problem in your country?

Possible answer: The biggest problem not just in my country but in the world is global warming. We're in the *calm before the storm* right now but I think we'll see the world get exponentially warmer in the coming years.

Can't make heads or tails of it

Meaning: Unable to understand something.

Origin: Probably goes back to Ancient Rome. Cicero used a phrase that meant neither head nor feet to refer to confusion.

Example IELTS question: Can you describe a time that you helped a friend?

Possible answer: Sure, I can remember a time in university that I helped a friend with an upcoming math exam. He *couldn't make heads or tails* of the material but we walked through it together, step by step and he ended up passing the test.

Can't put my finger on it

Meaning: Not sure exactly what is wrong.

Origin: From the 1800s. Refers to looking through a document and putting your finger onto something to support what you're looking for. If you can't find what you're looking for, then you can't put your finger on it.

Example IELTS question: How do you distinguish fake news from real news?
Possible answer: I mean, you often *can't put your finger on it* but it's a feeling you get when you're reading or looking at something. If it's too outside the norm, then people should check it against other resources to see if it matches up.

Cash in your chips

Meaning: Quit or stop.

Origin: From the 1900s. Gamblers turn in their chips for the cash equivalent when they're finished playing.

Example IELTS question: Describe a time when you made a good decision about something.
Possible answer: I'd like to talk about a good financial decision I made after the stock market crash in 2004. I had a lot of money invested and when the market crashed, lots of people *cashed in their chips* and took a big loss. But, I held on and even invested more money and stock prices have tripled now.

Caught between a rock and a hard place

Meaning: A difficult decision with two less than ideal options.

Origin: From Greek mythology. In the *Odyssey*, Odysseus had to pass between a treacherous whirlpool (the hard place) and a man-eating monster on a cliff (the rock).

Example IELTS question: Describe a piece of advice that you received recently.

Possible answer: I was talking to a good friend about a situation at work where there seemed like no good outcome. She said that you're *caught between a rock and a hard place* and to just ride it out and not do anything for a week or two. She was right and the situation resolved itself with time.

Caught me off guard

Meaning: Surprised me.

Origin: Unknown.

Example IELTS question: Do you usually celebrate your birthday?

Possible answer: I usually don't like to make a big deal about my birthday. But last year, my friends threw me a surprise birthday. It *caught me off guard* as I had no idea but to my surprise, I loved it.

Compare apples to oranges

Meaning: When people try to compare two things that shouldn't be compared because they're too different.

Origin: In use since the late 1800s. Predated by the idiom, "apples to oysters" in the 1600s as two things that could never be compared.

Example IELTS question: What is the difference between white-collar jobs and blue-collar jobs?

Possible answer: These days, comparing blue-collar and white-collar jobs is like *comparing apples to oranges*. Machines are doing more of the physical labour and repetitive tasks and many of the traditionally blue-collar jobs require using computers.

Cool as a cucumber

Meaning: Very calm or relaxed.

Origin: Unknown but cucumbers always feel cool and fresh inside, no matter how hot it is.

Example IELTS question: Did you have a favourite teacher from when you were growing up?

Possible answer: I still remember my grade 6 teacher, Mrs. Smith. We behaved so badly in her class but she was always *as cool as a cucumber* and never got angry! I can't believe she was so kind to us and by the end of the year, we all loved her.

Corner the market

Meaning: Gain a lot of the market share.

Origin: Unknown, but likely originated in the 1800s with the beginning of the market economy.

Example IELTS question: Describe a company whose products you love.

Possible answer: It's maybe a bit of a cliche, but I love Apple products. They have *cornered the market* in the personal computer and smartphone space because their products are so intuitive and also very high in quality. I find that they're far more durable than something from Dell or Toshiba, for example.

Costs an arm and a leg

Meaning: Very expensive; costs more than you can afford.

Origin: Uncertain but one theory is that it comes from painters in the 1700s. For portraits, the cheapest option was just the head and shoulders as painters charged more for arms and legs.

Example IELTS question: Do you prefer desktops or laptops?

Possible answer: I mostly use a computer for gaming but gaming laptops *cost an arm and a* *leg* so I generally stick with desktops.

Counting her chickens before they hatch

Meaning: Counting on something before it's already happened. For example, making plans to go to a certain university before getting the official acceptance letter.

Origin: First seen in the 1500s in Thomas Howell's *New Sonnets and Pretty Pamphlets*. Could have originated from medieval or Latin fables. Not all eggs hatch into chicks. Some are unfertilized or have another problem.

Example IELTS question: Describe a time when you got some good news.

Possible answer: I'm going to talk about getting into UBC. I got good grades in high school and met all the requirements but I'm not the type to *count my chickens before they hatch* so I still applied to some other universities. UBC was my first choice though. Anyway, I got in and now I'm going to graduate in just a few months.

Crack the whip

Meaning: To be tough on someone or encourage people to get to work.

Origin: Related to drivers of horse-drawn carriages who cracked their whips to get the horses to go faster. The first use of it related to people is seen in the 1800s.

Example IELTS question: What is a memory that you have from childhood?

Possible answer: I remember that my dad used to *crack the whip* on Saturday morning and make us clean up the house. But then he'd take us somewhere like the pool or the park as a reward.

Crunch the numbers

Meaning: Analyze data.

Origin: Came into use in the 1980s when computers became more commonplace and refers to the complicated numerical calculations that mainframe computers did at the time.

Example IELTS question: Describe something that you bought recently.

Possible answer: I bought a big thing recently—a condo! I wasn't sure I could afford it here in Vancouver but a mortgage broker *crunched the numbers* and made it work. I'm going to be moving in next month.

Cut to the chase

Meaning: Get to the most important thing.

Origin: Early films often finished with a chase scene. The early meaning meant to skip unnecessary dialogue and get to this more exciting part so that the audience wouldn't get bored.

Example IELTS question: Describe a time you've had to deal with a difficult person.

Possible answer: I had a boss who would beat around the bush and never give me any real direction about what I was supposed to be doing. I finally said something along the lines of, *cut to the chase*. Just tell me the three most important things I need to get done each day and I'll make sure I prioritize those things.

Don't see eye to eye

Meaning: Disagree with someone.

Origin: From Isaiah 52:8 in the Bible, "...for eye to eye they see the return of the Lord to Zion."

Example IELTS question: What's a memory that you have from your school days?

Possible answer: I remember one teacher and I just *didn't see eye to eye*. I think he had it in for me and I'd get in trouble for doing nothing! It got so bad that the principal finally switched me to another class.

Down on my luck

Meaning: Experiencing a period of bad times.

Origin: Somewhat uncertain but first seen in the 1800s to describe someone experiencing financial embarrassment, usually temporarily. Now can mean any kind of difficulty.

Example IELTS question: What are some pros and cons of school uniforms?

Possible answer: School uniforms are positive in that students don't feel pressure to follow the fashion trends. However, they can be quite expensive and are maybe a financial burden for families who are a bit *down on their luck*.

Fall through the cracks

Meaning: Overlook something.

Origin: Unknown. However, it's easy to imagine small cracks in old wooden floors and things going missing.

Example IELTS question: What can be done to alleviate poverty?

Possible answer: Poor people often *fall through the cracks* when it comes to things like medical and dental services. The government should provide free clinics for people who are unable to access these things.

Feeling the pinch

Meaning: Experiencing financial difficulties.

Origin: From the 1800s. Could be related to having to tighten a belt when there is less food to eat. Or, kids who have to wear shoes that are too small and getting their toes pinched because parents couldn't afford to buy new ones.

Example IELTS question: What social problems are there in your country?

Possible answer: The USA, like most countries, is *feeling the pinch* from Covid-19 and there's less money to go around for things like homeless or unemployed people. These problems are only going to get worse as time goes on.

Feeling under the weather

Meaning: Not feeling well; feeling sick.

Origin: Related to traveling by sea. People most often become seasick when the weather is bad. When this happened, they were sent below the deck, out of the weather and where the sway of the ship was less.

Example IELTS question: Do you think there will be less illness in the future?

Possible answer: People will always have periods of time where they *feel under the weather*. Technology is great at diagnosing or treating medical problems after they've already occurred but I'm not sure it works well for prevention.

Foot the bill

Meaning: To pay for something.

Origin: Comes from an early idiom in the 1500s, "foot up." It means to add up numbers on a bill and come to a total at the bottom (foot) of it. First seen as "foot the bill" in the 1800s.

Example IELTS question: Do you eat out at restaurants a lot?

Possible answer: Yes, I love to eat at restaurants as long as I'm not *footing the bill*! I'm a student so money is tight.

From rags to riches

Meaning: Going from poor to rich.

Origin: Uncertain but history is full of examples of people who did this.

Example IELTS question: Describe a movie that you've seen recently.

Possible answer: Sure, I recently watched _____. It was a *rags to riches* story about this guy who went from being homeless to starting his own business and then in turn, he helped a lot of other people get off the streets.

Get down to business

Meaning: Start working.

Origin: Unknown.

Example IELTS question: How do you usually spend your day at work?

Possible answer: Well, at work we start the day with a meeting to discuss the objectives for the day. Then we *get down to business* with whatever task has been assigned to each person.

Get into deep water

Meaning: To be in trouble.

Origin: From Psalm 69:14 in the Bible, "...out of the deep waters."

Example IELTS question: Do you think that most companies are ethical?

Possible answer: There are some good companies out there but if you look at the news, there are always stories of businesses *getting into deep water* for one reason or the other.

Get in touch with

Meaning: Contact someone.

Origin: Could be from the 1800s where soldiers in military marches had to be close enough so that they could touch the person next to them.

Example IELTS question: What are some things that you do online?

Possible answer: One of my favourite things that I use the Internet for is to get in touch with friends and family members. I love seeing what my nieces and nephews are up to on Facebook or Instagram.

Get my foot in the door

Meaning: Achieve some initial stage. For example, an entry-level job at a company.

Origin: Related to the selling tactics of door-to-door salespeople. They try to get one foot inside the door to make it impossible for the homeowner to shut it so that they can continue their sales pitch.

Example IELTS question: How long have you been working at your current job?

Possible answer: I haven't been there long, just a few months now. I did an internship there in university which helped me *get my foot in the door* for a full-time job.

Getting on in years

Meaning: Becoming older.

Origin: Unknown.

Example IELTS question: How do you spend your weekends?

Possible answer: Well, my parents are *getting on in years* so I usually go over to their house and help them out. Things like mowing the lawn or picking up groceries. They don't get around as easily as they used to.

Get up to speed

Meaning: Achieve competence at something or to be fully informed.

Origin: First seen in the 1800s to refer to something that had the power to achieve an optimal working speed such as a horse or a machine. Later, during the Apollo-13 mission and the Watergate hearings of the 1970s, it meant to be fully informed.

Example IELTS question: What's your job like?

Possible answer: Well, I just started at this company so I'm still *getting up to speed*. I'll be officially done training next week so I'll have a better idea then what every day will be like.

Give her a ring

Meaning: Call someone by phone.

Origin: First seen in the early 1900s when telephones came into common usage.

Example IELTS question: Describe a time when you helped someone.

Possible answer: I remember when I was a teenager and I just got my driver's license. My mom had an older friend who was quite sick with cancer treatments so she asked me to help her out. The friend would *give me a ring* and ask me to do this or that, like pick up her medications or some groceries.

Give him the cold shoulder

Meaning: Ignore someone.

Origin: Somewhat unknown but could be from a mistranslation of a Latin phrase in Nehemiah 9:29 in the Vulgate Bible.

Example IELTS question: Do you have any negative memories from your school days?

Possible answer: I remember in middle school when I missed a few weeks of school because I was in the hospital. When I came back, my friends *gave me the cold shoulder* for some reason or another. It was very hurtful as we'd been friends since kindergarten.

Give them a run for their money

Meaning: Provide good competition.

Origin: Could be from horse racing and placing bets. Sometimes horses are withdrawn from a race after bets are placed in which case you don't get a run for your money.

Example IELTS question: Is there a certain brand of technology that you like using?

Possible answer: Sure, like most people, I love my iPhone. However, Samsung is starting to *give them a run for their money* these days so I may switch to them for my next one.

Go for broke

Meaning: To risk everything in one final effort or push.

Origin: From Hawaiian Pidgin slang. Refers to gambling when you wager everything on a single roll in craps.

Example IELTS question: Have you ever done something really difficult?

Possible answer: I did a triathlon a few years ago and didn't do as well as I'd hoped on the swimming portion so I ended up having to *go for broke* on the run, pushing myself much harder than I normally would. The good news is that I ended up placing third in my age category.

Good head on your shoulders

Meaning: Smart or intelligent.

Origin: First seen in the 1500s to refer to an old head on young shoulders (physical youth combined with wisdom).

Example IELTS question: Are there any celebrities that you follow?

Possible answer: I admire Meghan Markle who's married to Prince Harry. She's a talented actress but also seems like she has a *good head on her shoulders.*

Go out on a limb

Meaning: To take a risk.

Origin: Related to climbing trees and going out a bit further on a branch (limb) than is comfortable. First seen in writing in the late 1890s in the USA.

Example IELTS question: Do you prefer using a desktop or a laptop computer?

Possible answer: I'm going to go out on a limb here and say neither! I usually use my Smartphone for just about everything. I borrow my son's computer once in a while for taxes or something like that though.

Go the extra mile

Meaning: Work very hard to do a good job. Doing something extra than is expected.

Origin: From Matthew 5:41 in the Bible. Under Roman law, a soldier could order a Jew to carry his pack for a mile. Matthew said to carry it even further than that without complaint.

Example IELTS question: What are some qualities of a good employee.

Possible answer: The best quality of a good employee is someone that will *go the extra mile* to get the job done. This applies to any job or industry. If someone doesn't care about results for the company, they will only do the bare minimum.

Got a taste of his own medicine

Meaning: Being treated in the same bad way he/she has treated other people.

Origin: Comes from Aesop's famous story when a swindler sells fake medicine to lots of people, claiming it could help them. When he gets sick, people give him his own medicine which of course, doesn't work.

Example IELTS question: Describe something that you've read recently.

Possible answer: I was reading a story with my son last night before bed. It was about this kid who was a bit of a bully at school. He started picking on one particular child and it went into lots of details about that. But in the end, he *got a taste of his own medicine* and understood how his actions were wrong.

Got up on the wrong side of the bed

Meaning: Someone who is grumpy.

Origin: From ancient Rome. They had a superstition that said getting up on the left side of the bed would bring them bad luck for the day.

Example IELTS question: What's a normal morning like for you?

Possible answer: It kind of depends on the day and if my son *gets up on the wrong side of the bed*, or not! If he doesn't, then it goes quite smoothly as I get ready for work and get him ready for school. If he does, it's a struggle and we both end up being almost late. He doesn't want to cooperate with me for anything.

Got started off on the wrong foot

Meaning: Get started badly.

Origin: Unclear but in use since the 1600s. One theory is that it refers to the left foot which is not most people's dominant foot. Another theory is that it refers to military marches where everyone has to start with the same foot to be in sync.

Example IELTS question: What's it like working at your company?

Possible answer: It's pretty relaxed and I generally enjoy my job. One of my coworkers and I *got started off on the wrong foot* so it was stressful in the beginning but that's resolved now.

Got wind of

Meaning: Heard about a certain thing.

Origin: Used since the early 1800s. Refers to animals who become aware of scents that are carried in the air.

Example IELTS question: Do you follow celebrity gossip?

Possible answer: Never, it's a total waste of time I think and I think that probably 99% of it isn't true. If there's anything that's big news, my friend will tell me. The other day, she *got wind of*. . .

Go with the flow

Meaning: To relax and go along with whatever happens.

Origin: Used by the Roman Emperor Marcus Aurelius who said that it was better to go with the flow than to try to change society.

Example IELTS question: How can a company develop more leaders in their organization?

Possible answer: First of all, not everyone needs to be a leader. There need to be people in any organization who just *go with the flow* and follow directions well. As far as developing leaders, it's usually best to develop them from within because these people know the corporate culture.

Hit the books

Meaning: Study.

Origin: Unknown.

Example IELTS question: What do you usually do in the evenings?

Possible answer: I know it's kind of boring but in the evenings, I usually *hit the books*. I'm trying to become a chartered accountant and am doing classes at nights and on weekends.

Hit the ground running

Meaning: Start something and make progress quickly on it.

Origin: Unknown but could be related to soldiers who are dropped by parachute into combat zones and have to be ready to fight the second they hit the ground. Or, could refer to stowaways who jump off a train when it gets close to the station and have to begin running to avoid the police.

Example IELTS question: What's your usual morning routine?

Possible answer: I have a very long commute so I usually have to *hit the ground running* as soon as my alarm goes off. I take a quick shower, grab breakfast and coffee for the road and then start driving to work.

Hit the nail on the head

Meaning: See the problem clearly and precisely.

Origin: Related to carpentry. You want to hit the nail squarely on the head to avoid damaging the thing you're working on or yourself.

Example IELTS question: Did you spend time with your grandparents growing up?

Possible answer: I spent a lot of time with my paternal grandfather and I enjoyed it. I'd always talk to him about some issues I was having and he'd always *hit the nail on the head* with his advice.

Hold the purse strings

Meaning: Make financial decisions.

Origin: Unknown.

Example IELTS question: Describe something that you've bought recently.

Possible answer: In my house, my wife *holds the purse strings* so she makes most of the daily spending decisions. However, we decided to buy an RV so we did lots of research and then spent months looking for the perfect one.

I'll have to see it to believe it

Meaning: When you don't think something is likely or believable and you want to see it with your own eyes.

Origin: Unknown.

Example IELTS question: Do you waste time doing things online?

Possible answer: I sometimes feel I'm wasting my life away looking at videos on TikTok! I'm a sucker for the headlines that seem so unbelievable and then I think, *I'll have to see it to believe it* so of course, I watch.

In it for the long haul

Meaning: Committed to something or someone for the long term.

Origin: Somewhat unknown but could be related to the fact that strategy for a long journey or project is different from a short-term one.

Example IELTS question: Do you like your job?

Possible answer: My job has its up and downs for sure but I'm *in it for the long haul*. I want to make partner and I'm only a couple of years away I think.

In the dog house

Meaning: In trouble.

Origin: First seen in *Peter Pan* in 1911 when the father stays in the dog's kennel to express his remorse for causing his children to be kidnapped.

Example IELTS question: What do you usually do on the weekends?

Possible answer: It kind of depends if my children are *in the dog house*, or not. If they haven't done their chores or homework for the week, they have to finish that before going out to do anything fun. If they have, then we usually plan a fun outing like going to the lake or a movie.

In the driver's seat

Meaning: In control of something; able to make decisions.

Origin: First seen in the 1600s with "In the saddle." "In the driver's seat" came into common usage in the 1800s when cars became more popular.

Example IELTS question: Describe a time when you had to make a difficult decision.

Possible answer: After university, I was fortunate enough to have three job offers. I was *in the driver's seat* but it wasn't easy to choose between them. In the end, I went with the company offering the highest salary which I think was the correct decision.

In the same boat

Meaning: In a similar situation as someone else; or a situation where peoples' fates are tied together.

Origin: Various theories but one is that it was used by the ancient Greeks to refer to all the people in a boat facing the same fate when going out to sea. They would all either survive and make it, or sink and drown.

Example IELTS question: Are most people addicted to social media?

Possible answer: Oh, we're all *in the same boat*—totally addicted! I watched a documentary about how companies like Facebook or Instagram design their platforms to be addictive.

It's a long shot

Meaning: Something that's not likely to happen.

Origin: From the 1700s to refer to the chance of hitting a target with a gun or arrow that is very far away. In the 1800s came into common usage with horse racing to refer to a horse that had only a small chance of winning.

Example IELTS question: How did you get your current job?

Possible answer: I heard an ad for it on the radio and just applied. I know *it was a long shot* but it ended up working out.

It's not rocket science

Meaning: Something that shouldn't be that difficult to do.

Origin: Came into common usage in 1980 as rocket science is considered to be something difficult to master. Before this, the common phrase was, "It's not brain surgery."

Example IELTS question: Do you find your work challenging?

Possible answer: *It's not rocket science*, that's for sure! But, there are small ways in which I can increase efficiency so I challenge myself to do that.

It's time to face the music

Meaning: Deal with the reality of something bad that you did. For example, getting punished for a crime.

Origin: From the USA in the early 1800s. Various theories:

 – Related to stage fright.

 – Related to the drumbeat that was played when a soldier was removed from the military for bad behaviour.

 – Related to a soldier going into battle to face the music of the opponent's guns.

Example IELTS question: Is corruption a big problem in your country?

Possible answer: There's lots of corruption in _____. *It's time* for some of the big companies *to face the music* and pay their fair share of taxes.

It takes two to tango

Meaning: There are two people responsible for a situation or problem.

Origin: First came into common usage with the 1952 song by Al Hoffman and Dick Manning, "*Takes Two to Tango.*"

Example IELTS question: Do labour unions play an important role in your country?

Possible answer: Not really and I don't think they're needed. *It takes two to tango*, right? Employees can just find another job if they don't like the salary or conditions at their current job. The minimum labour standards set out by the government are quite robust.

I've got my work cut out for me

Meaning: A big or difficult job to do.

Origin: Goes back to the 1600s. A good tailor (someone who makes clothes) would have everything cut out before starting to sew. Successful tailors would hire someone to do the cutting for them.

Example IELTS question: How do you usually spend your weekends?

Possible answer: I work almost 80 hours during the week in the film industry, so *I've got my work cut out for me* on the weekends with stuff to do around the house. My kids have dental appointments or hair cuts and I have to do all the lawn and car maintenance as well.

Jumping on the bandwagon

Meaning: Following the crowd or popular opinion.

Origin: First seen in 1848 in the USA when a famous circus clown used his bandwagon to gain attention for his political campaign appearances. It became popular and other politicians wanted to jump (get a seat) on his bandwagon.

Example IELTS question: Is there a brand that is very well-known in your country?

Possible answer: Everyone loves Apple products, such as their laptops or phones. It's not just people *jumping on the bandwagon* though. In my experience, they are top-quality products that are backed up by excellent customer service.

Keep me in the loop

Meaning: Update me; keep me informed.

Origin: Comes from the military where orders are passed in a feedback loop so everyone is well-informed.

Example IELTS question: Describe one of your friends.

Possible answer: I'd like to talk about my friend Terry. We get along so well because she's funny and I'm always happy when I'm hanging out with her. She also likes me to *keep her in the loop* about my dating life and all the other things happening so we text a lot too. I just get the feeling that she cares a lot about what happens in my life and I feel the same way about her.

Keep me on my toes

Meaning: Always ready to deal with anything that might happen. A situation or person that is challenging and requires someone to be at their best to handle it.

Origin: Various explanations. One of them relates to short people having to stand on their toes to see something when in a crowd of people.

Example IELTS question: What do you usually do in the evening?

Possible answer: After I come home from work, I take over with the kids to give my husband a break. They *keep me on my toes*—they're 3 and 6 so are very active.

Keep this under wraps

Meaning: Not tell anyone; conceal something.

Origin: From horse racing in the late 1800s. Refers to slowing down a horse by wrapping the reins around the hand in the beginning and middle of a race to hide the true speed. Then, they will have the strength for a sudden burst of energy at the end as they cross the finish line.

Example IELTS question: Do you think stronger privacy laws in your country are necessary?

Possible answer: Not at all. In Canada, I sometimes think privacy laws are too strong. Some things shouldn't be *kept under wraps* in the interest of public safety for example.

Keep your eye on the prize

Meaning: Remember the most important thing.

Origin: From a folk song that became popular during the civil rights movement in the USA in the 1950s and 1960s.

Example IELTS question: Describe a time when someone gave you some good or bad advice.

Possible answer: I remember when I was in my last year of university and I was very busy with an internship, a part-time job and all of my classes as well. I was talking to my mom about giving up but she told me to *keep my eye on the prize* and that it'd all be over in a few months. She was right and I did end up finishing my degree.

Keep your head above water

Meaning: Trying to just break even. Having a hard time with something difficult.

Origin: Unknown but is likely related to struggling to keep your head above water so that you don't drown.

Example IELTS question: Are you usually quite busy at work?

Possible answer: It depends on the time of year. Around the holidays, we struggle to *keep our heads above wate*r but then it slows down in January.

Kick back and relax

Meaning: Chill out.

Origin: Came into popular use in the late 1900s.

Example IELTS question: What do you enjoy doing on holidays?

Possible answer: I love to just *kick back and relax*. It doesn't matter where I am. It could be the beach, the mountains or just at home.

Land on your feet

Meaning: To be in a good position again after a difficult time.

Origin: Unknown.

Example IELTS question: Do you think that the government provides enough social safety nets in your country?

Possible answer: Yes, most definitely. Sweden has several programs to help the working poor and the unemployed. Anyone who wants to *land on their feet* can usually do so.

Learn the ropes

Meaning: Get trained to do something.

Origin: Two possible explanations. The first is from people who travelled around doing rope tricks for a living. These tricks were not easy to learn and master. The second is new sailors who had to learn to tie ropes on sailing ships.

Example IELTS question: What is a difficult job?

Possible answer: I think that one of the most difficult jobs is being a doctor. It takes a long time to *learn the ropes*, and then after that, you have so much responsibility. One mistake could result in someone dying.

Let off the hook

Meaning: To not be punished, even though he/she was caught doing something wrong. For example, a politician who doesn't go to jail even though he committed a crime.

Origin: From the 1800s and refers to a fish letting themselves off a hook to not be caught.

Example IELTS question: Do you think the punishment for criminals in your country is strong enough?

Possible answer: In general, it's fair for crimes that cause physical harm. However, politicians often get *let off the hook* way too easily for things like corruption.

Like riding a bike

Meaning: Something that you always remember how to do, even with a large break of time in between.

Origin: Unknown but came into usage sometime after 1860 when people started using the word bicycle.

Example IELTS question: Do you play a musical instrument?

Possible answer: I used to play the piano quite well when I was a kid. I stopped for many years but picked it up again quite recently. It was *like riding a bike*. I was surprised by how much I remembered.

Like two peas in a pod

Meaning: Two people who are very similar in thinking or appearance.

Origin: Refers to peas still in the peapod that are almost identical in size and color.

Example IELTS question: Do you miss your high-school life?

Possible answer: I loved high school. My best friend Jenny and I were *like two peas in a pod* and always getting into trouble together!

Living hand to mouth

Meaning: Live paycheck to paycheck. Not having lots of money, especially disposable income.

Origin: Goes back to the 1600s and may have referred to a time of famine in England.

Example IELTS question: Is homelessness a problem in your country?

Possible answer: It's not a huge problem as the government provides subsidized housing for anyone who needs it. However, there are a lot of working poor who are *living hand to mouth* and are one small crisis from financial disaster.

Looks like a million bucks

Meaning: Look attractive or well put together.

Origin: Unknown, but in the days when you could buy a hamburger or soda for $0.05, a million bucks (dollars) was a lot of money. A million dollars was considered to be very wealthy.

Example IELTS question: Who is your favourite celebrity?

Possible answer: My favourite celebrity is Tom Cruise and I never miss any of his movies. He *looks like a million bucks* too, despite getting on in years.

Make a break for it

Meaning: Leave somewhere quickly.

Origin: Unknown.

Example IELTS question: Do you like outdoor activities?

Possible answer: Yes, I love anything outside. I joke with my boss on nice days about *making a break for it* when he isn't looking!

Making a mountain out of a molehill

Meaning: To make something into a bigger deal than it is. For example, someone who gets a traffic ticket but doesn't pay it and then ends up going to jail because of it.

Origin: From the 1500s in Nicholas Udall's translation of "*The First Tome or Volume of the Paraphrase of Erasmus upon the New Testament.*"

Example IELTS question: Do you think social media platforms should be subject to censorship?

Possible answer: Honestly, no. It's quite obvious what's fake news and what isn't. People that are clamouring for this are just *making a mountain out of a molehill.*

Make ends meet

Meaning: Make enough money to pay all the bills.

Origin: First seen in the 1600s but the origin is uncertain.

Example IELTS question: Do you think that government should be doing more to protect the environment?

Possible answer: There are two sides to it. On the one hand, lots of people are struggling to *make ends meet* and the government should be doing more to help them. But, the longer-term issue is global warming which needs to be addressed as well.

Make some bank (Make bank)

Meaning: To earn lots of money.

Origin: Uncertain but first seen in the 2000s. Common in rap songs.

Example IELTS question: Is a high-paying job always a good job?

Possible answer: Not at all! Even though someone might *make bank* being a lawyer or an accountant, they might have to work 100 hours a week for it and it wouldn't be worth it. You have to have time to enjoy the money that you make!

Missed the boat

Meaning: To perform poorly or badly.

Origin: A common expression in England in the 1700s when boat transport was the main way to get around. To miss the boat meant that you were stuck having to wait for the next one, missing out on opportunities.

Example IELTS question: What do you think we can learn by studying history?

Possible answer: We can learn what to avoid in the future by studying the past. All countries have *missed the boat* in one way or the other about important things so hopefully, these things can be avoided again.

Money burning a hole in your pocket

Meaning: Extra money that you want to spend.

Origin: A similar phrase was used as early as the 1500s and the current one was seen in the 1800s.

Example IELTS question: Do you like spending or saving money?

Possible answer: I'm a spender. Whenever I get paid, I feel like I have *money burning a hole* *in my pocket* and I go shopping!

Money to burn

Meaning: Extra money to spend freely.

Origin: Used since the 1800s and refers to paper money that you don't need. Hence, you can afford to light it on fire and burn or waste it.

Example IELTS question: Do you think we should let children spend money they get however they want?

Possible answer: I know children feel like they have *money to burn* around their birthday or Christmas. However, parents should teach kids about the importance of saving some for a rainy day as well.

My hands are tied

Meaning: Unable to do something, even if you wanted to.

Origin: First seen in the 1600s. Refers to being unable to do something because someone else has tied your hands together.

Example IELTS question: Do you think parents spend too much on toys and gadgets for their children?

Possible answer: In general, yes. However, their *hands are tied* if everyone has a certain toy or gadget and you don't want your own kid to feel left out or excluded. This is especially true for teenagers who have a strong need to fit in with their peers at school.

Needle in a haystack

Meaning: Something that is impossible to find.

Origin: In ancient times, needles were made from bone or wood and looked similar to hay.

This made them very difficult to find in a big haystack.

Example IELTS question: In your opinion, why do some people like shopping at secondhand stores?

Possible answer: People like shopping there because when you get something good for a cheap price, it's like finding a *needle in a haystack*. Some people get an adrenaline rush from it I think.

Nip this in the bud

Meaning: To stop something bad from happening early on in the process.
Origin: First seen in the early 1600s and describes the de-budding of plants that were nipped off.

Example IELTS question: For parents, what is important in bringing up children?

Possible answer: Parents have a responsibility to raise children who will contribute meaningfully to society. They should also *nip negative behaviours in the bud*. I mean things like stealing or lying.

No pain, no gain

Meaning: Working hard for something, undergoing hardship because of it.
Origin: Came into popular use in 1982. Jane Fonda used the saying in her popular workout videos.

Example IELTS question: Do you enjoy exercise?

Possible answer: Not really but as they say, *no pain, no gain*! I hit the gym a few times a week to stay in shape.

Not going to fly

Meaning: Not going to work.

Origin: First seen in the late 1800s with the development of airplanes.

Example IELTS question: What is the general attitude towards people arriving late in your country?

Possible answer: In social settings, it's generally acceptable to arrive a few minutes late. However, for work, it's *not going to fly*. You need to arrive at least a few minutes early in most cases.

Not my cup of tea

Meaning: Not something I like or would do. For example, you have a friend who loves skydiving but you have no interest in it.

Origin: First seen in the late 1800s in England as "My cup of tea" to describe something you enjoyed. A few years later, "Not" was added to describe something you don't like.

Example IELTS question: Do you like travelling by boat?

Possible answer: Travelling by boat is *not my cup of tea*. I will usually drive or take the plane if at all possible.

Not seeing the forest for the trees

Meaning: Seeing only small details instead of the big picture.

Origin: First seen in the 1500s in the *Proverbs of John Heywood*.

Example IELTS question: Should the government do more to encourage recycling?

Possible answer: Yes, but I think that as a society, we're *not seeing the forest for the trees*. We should be focusing on consuming fewer things instead of recycling all the junk!

Not set in stone

Meaning: Not decided 100% yet.

Origin: Came into popular use in the 1700s when tombstones were made from stone or granite. Carving or writing something into them is permanent, as compared to something like wood.

Example IELTS question: In your country, is it okay to arrive late for things?

Possible answer: Where I'm from, *nothing* is *set in stone* in terms of time. If the bus is supposed to leave at 1:00, it may leave at 1:30 or even 2:00. We are just way more relaxed about things like this than in the USA or Canada.

Off his rocker

Meaning: Someone who is acting crazy or not rationally.

Origin: Rocking chairs were very common in the 1800s and people often socialized with neighbors while enjoying some beers. Inevitably, someone would get drunk and fall out of the rocking chair (off his rocker).

Example IELTS question: Do you follow the news closely?

Possible answer: I like to keep tabs on what's happening in politics. For example, I was fascinated by Donald Trump *going off his rocker* while he was president.

Off the top of my head

Meaning: Without research or deep thought about something.

Origin: First seen in the mid-1900s but not much else is known besides that. Could be related to coming to a conclusion about something without using your entire brainpower.

Example IELTS question: What are the traditional art forms in your country?

Possible answer: Well, *off the top of my head*, I don't know much about art. But, I think masks are quite a common kind of art where I'm from.

Once in a blue moon

Meaning: Something that doesn't happen often.

Origin: First seen in 1528 in an anti-Church pamphlet. The reference to the blue moon is a conversation between two characters saying that if someone tells you that the moon is blue, you must believe it. The Church at that time was making outrageous statements and expecting people to believe them.

Example IELTS question: Do you watch sports on TV?

Possible answer: Only *once in a blue moon*. I watch the Olympics and then the World Cup if Germany is playing.

Out of the loop

Meaning: Not knowing anything.

Origin: Comes from the military where orders are passed in a feedback loop so everyone is informed.

Example IELTS question: Do you follow the news closely?

Possible answer: To be honest, I'm a bit *out of the loop* when it comes to what's happening in the world. I rely on friends posting important things on Facebook.

Out of my depth

Meaning: Not qualified for, lacks knowledge of.

Origin: Unknown.

Example IELTS question: Do you think there will be less illness in the future?

Possible answer: I'm a bit out of my depth here and don't know that much about health or preventing illness. However, I'd assume that with better technology, we may get better at preventing and also treating illnesses.

Paying through the nose

Meaning: Paying too much or more than usual for something.

Origin: Uncertain but could be related to when the Danes conquered Ireland in the 800s and took a census by counting noses. A large tax was imposed on each person (nose).

Example IELTS question: Do you ever give greetings cards to people?

Possible answer: I'm pretty frugal so I hate having to *pay through the nose* for a piece of paper that people are going to throw into the trash. I generally just give the gift wrapped in brown paper and then I write my note on that!

Pick up the slack

Meaning: Working harder out of necessity because someone else isn't working hard enough.

Origin: Related to working on ships where you'd have to fix a portion of a rope that hung too loosely by "picking up the slack." The opposite idiom is "Cut some slack."

Example IELTS question: Are you pretty busy on the weekends?

Possible answer: Well, my husband works weekends so I'm at home alone with the kids all weekend so have to *pick up the slack*. I'm usually so busy that I don't even have time to think.

Playing catch up

Meaning: To try to reach the same level as others, especially after starting late.

Origin: Dates back to the 1800s. One theory is that it was commonly used in sports such as football to describe a team that was losing.

Example IELTS question: Are you good at saving money?

Possible answer: I used to be terrible at saving money but now that I'm in my forties, I'm trying to *play catch up* for all those years that I was a free spender.

Pull the plug

Meaning: Stop or cancel something before it's finished.

Origin: A medical term related to unplugging a life support or breathing machine that is keeping someone alive. To turn off the machine (pull the plug) means that the person will die.

Example IELTS question: Describe an unexpected event.

Possible answer: Last summer, I went camping in Lytton and there was a big thunderstorm that caused some wildfires to start. They were quite small to start with but they started to spread rapidly and we had to *pull the plug* on the trip. We were barely able to pack up everything before we started to see the fires right close to us.

Pull the wool over my eyes

Meaning: Trick someone.

Origin: First seen in the USA in the 1800s and probably comes from people commonly wearing wigs made out of wool.

Example IELTS question: What's a good memory that you have from childhood?

Possible answer: My brother and I used to *pull the wool over my parents' eyes* and get away with murder. Now that I look back on it though, I think my parents maybe did know what we were doing, but they just let us get away with it!

Put all your eggs in one basket

Meaning: Count on only one thing to work out; to explore only one option.

Origin: Uncertain but one of the earliest uses was in the book, *Don Quixote* by Miguel Cervantes.

Example IELTS question: What's your favourite shop?

Possible answer: I'm not the type to *put all my eggs in one basket* so I have a few places that I like to go, depending on the various sales. And some places are best for jeans, others for electronics, others for gifts. Of course, I always compare prices with online sites like Amazon as well for any big purchase.

Put my best foot forward

Meaning: To be on one's best behaviour.

Origin: First seen in a poem dating from 1613, *A Wife* by Thomas Overbury.

Example IELTS question: Is being fashionable important to you?

Possible answer: Sure, I like to *put my best foot forward* so I will usually put some effort into what I wear when leaving my house.

Put your money where your mouth is

Meaning: Actions need to reflect words.

Origin: First seen in the 1930s in the USA, concerning backing up your words with cash.

Example IELTS question: Do people have respect for politicians in your country?

Possible answer: Almost none at all! Corruption is rampant and they are generally just all talk. I'm waiting for the day when someone *puts their money where their mouth is*, but it hasn't happened yet.

Put the cart before the horse

Meaning: Getting one or more steps ahead by skipping something important.

Origin: First seen in the 1500s when people commonly travelled by cart and horse. They could only go with the horse before the cart and not the other way around.

Example IELTS question: Are there recycling programs in your country?

Possible answer: Yes, but I think that's *putting the cart before the horse*. The local government has recently started a public education campaign about minimalism and buying fewer things.

Quit cold turkey

Meaning: Suddenly stop doing something addictive. Most commonly refers to smoking.

Origin: Various uses but first seen in the early 1900s regarding drug withdrawal.

Example IELTS question: Are you a generally healthy person?

Possible answer: I used to smoke almost a pack a day but I *quit cold turkey* about two years ago. Since then, I've been feeling better and better.

Race against the clock

Meaning: Time is running out to finish something.

Origin: First seen in the 1950s in sporting competitions where people don't directly compete against each other but are timed. For example, a time trial in cycling.

Example IELTS question: Are you concerned about the environment?

Possible answer: Definitely. We're in a race against the clock when it comes to global warming. I think that the Earth could become uninhabitable in just a few decades if we don't take action now.

Rally the troops

Meaning: Organize or convince people to do something.

Origin: Uncertain but the original usage was likely related to a military leader exhorting his soldiers before a battle.

Example IELTS question: Do you like hosting parties?

Possible answer: I have quite a small apartment so I generally don't have people over. But, I do like to *rally the troops* to try some restaurants in my neighborhood every month or two.

Read between the lines

Meaning: Discovering something secret or hidden.

Origin: First seen in the 1800s and refers to the hiding of secret messages or meanings between lines of text in a document.

Example IELTS question: Do you believe everything you see on the news?

Possible answer: Definitely not. I find that you have to *read between the lines* and also compare various accounts of the same story to get to the heart of any matter.

Rock the boat

Meaning: Cause trouble or make waves.

Origin: Attributed to American politician William Jennings Bryan in 1914. He used it to refer to those who stir up trouble.

Example IELTS question: Do you think that politicians do a good job in your country?

Possible answer: In Canada, they do a decent job and there isn't a lot of corruption like in other countries. However, they're also scared to *rock the boat* which prevents any sort of real change from happening.

Rule of thumb

Meaning: General rule about something.

Origin: Various theories:

- Builders who don't measure well and just use an approximate measure (thumb).

- A thumb is generally equivalent to an inch when measuring cloth.

- The thumb is used when brewing beer to gauge temperature.

- An alleged British law that allowed men to beat their wives with sticks no wider than a thumb.

Example IELTS question: Do you think children should get an allowance?

Possible answer: Kids should have some spending money so that they have a chance to practice spending and saving. But, a good *rule of thumb* is that parents should require them to save at least a little bit of it for the future.

Running around in circles

Meaning: Taking lots of action but not achieving anything.

Origin: Uncertain.

Example IELTS question: What do you usually do in the evenings?

Possible answer: I'm usually *running around in circles*, cleaning up after my kids, cooking dinner and putting them to bed. I can only rest when they're sleeping!

Same old, same old
Meaning: Nothing has changed.

Origin: First came into common use in the 1970s. It perhaps came from Pidgin English spoken in post-WWII Japan or Korea after the Korean war.

Example IELTS question: Do you feel optimistic about the future of your country?

Possible answer: I don't feel optimistic but I don't feel pessimistic either. Not that much changes from year to year. It's mostly just the *same old, same old*.

Selling like hotcakes

Meaning: Selling quickly.

Origin: Unclear but may be related to the fact that hotcakes (pancakes) were popular items at fairs and sold out quickly.

Example IELTS question: Do you like having the latest gadgets?

Possible answer: I know that whenever the new iPhone comes out, it *sells like hotcakes* but I honestly can't be bothered with that kind of thing. I just use whatever I have for years until it breaks.

Shake things up

Meaning: To reorganize something in a drastic or big way.

Origin: Uncertain.

Example IELTS question: How can a teacher make lessons for children more interesting?

Possible answer: Everything a teacher can do to *shake things up* will go a long way towards keeping children interested in lessons. However, routine is good too. I guess a balance between those two things is the best way.

Shop till she drops

Meaning: Loves shopping and spends lots of time doing it.

Origin: Seen as early as 1920 when it was used as an advertising slogan.

Example IELTS question: Do you like shopping?

Possible answer: I love to *shop till I drop*! It's my favourite hobby but the only problem is that I don't have a lot of money to spend.

Sick as a dog

Meaning: Very unwell.

Origin: Seen as early as the 1700s when people compared bad things to dogs and other animals. This is because they often carried disease.

Example IELTS question: Did you spend time with your extended family for the last holiday?

Possible answer: I generally do but around Christmas this year, I was *as sick as a dog* and stayed in bed for almost a week. Unfortunately, I had to miss all the family celebrations.

Smoke and mirrors

Meaning: Flashy things that distract from what is real.

Origin: Seen around the 1770s. Magicians used smoke and mirrors to create illusions.

Example IELTS question: Do you think that the government has a responsibility to protect people from scams and cyber-crime?

Possible answer: Yes, ideally they would protect people from this kind of thing, especially children and the elderly. They do to some degree but criminals are good at using *smoke and mirrors* so you never really know what's true, or not.

Spice things up

Meaning: To make things more interesting or exciting.

Origin: Uncertain.

Example IELTS question: What kind of food do you like to eat?

Possible answer: I'm a meat and potatoes kind of guy but if I like to *spice things up,* I'll go out for some Korean or Chinese.

Spill the beans

Meaning: Tell a secret.

Origin: It's thought to have originated in Ancient Greece. People used white or black beans to vote secretly. Then, the beans were spilled to reveal the results.

Example IELTS question: Have you ever had to keep a secret?

Possible answer: Yes, I found out that my sister had gotten engaged before the rest of my family did. It was so difficult to not *spill the beans* to everybody.

Stabbed someone in the back

Meaning: To betray someone, especially someone with a close relationship.

Origin: From Germany after WWI. The German army felt betrayed by politicians who signed the peace treaty because they thought they could win. Adolph Hitler used this "stabbed in the back" story during his rise to power to gain followers.

Example IELTS question: Describe one of your favourite films.

Possible answer: I love _____ and have seen it about 10 times now. It's a story of a guy who *stabbed his best friend in the back* and then in the end, his friend gets revenge and ends up even better off than he was before that happened.

Stealing my thunder

Meaning: Taking credit for something that someone else did.

Origin: From the early 1700s. A playwright invented a thunder machine and a few days later, someone stole the idea and used it in another play.

Example IELTS question: Do you get along well with your coworkers?

Possible answer: For the most part, I like them except for one person on my team. She's always *stealing my thunder* for ideas that I come up with and claiming that she had a big part in them. I've talked with her about it but she refuses to change her behaviour.

Step up to the plate

Meaning: Take responsibility.

Origin: Comes from baseball where the batter steps up to the home plate to hit the ball.

Example IELTS question: Should children be allowed to watch a lot of TV?

Possible answer: I think parents should *step up to the plate* and limit how much TV their children watch. It can impact brain development. I know that's easier said than done though!

Strapped for cash

Meaning: Lacking money.

Origin: From the mid-1800s when strapped used to refer to lack of cash.

Example IELTS question: Are you a spender or a saver?

Possible answer: I'm generally a spender but in my younger days, I was *strapped for cash* a lot so I'm capable of saving money if I have to!

Take a breather

Meaning: Relax for a while.

Origin: Unknown but likely related to exercise and breathing more heavily than usual.

Example IELTS question: Do you enjoy going on holidays?

Possible answer: Sure, but it's sometimes a lot of work to plan everything and get all packed up to go. Sometimes I like to take a staycation at home and just *take a breather* and slow down from normal life.

Taken to the cleaners

Meaning: Not doing well, struggling; someone took advantage of you.

Origin: Related to the earlier idiom, "To clean someone out." Taken to the cleaners came into use in the 1920s when dry cleaning shops began to appear.

Example IELTS question: Do you enjoy watching sports on TV?

Possible answer: I'm a big fan of the Edmonton Oilers but they got *taken to the cleaners* during playoffs by Winnipeg so I didn't enjoy that at all!

Take the bull by the horns

Meaning: Do something bravely and decisively.

Origin: Could be related to bullfighting in Europe, or cowboys in the USA who wrestled cows with horns.

Example IELTS question: Do you like to be a leader or a follower?

Possible answer: I like to *take the bull by the horns* and lead if it all possible. I'm the person among all my friends who is always planning trips or outings.

The ball's in your court

Meaning: You have the power to decide on something.

Origin: First came into use in the 1960s from tennis. When the ball is in your court, you must hit it back to keep the point going.

Example IELTS question: Do people do enough to protect the environment in your country?

Possible answer: To some degree, yes. Individuals do a pretty good job of things like recycling but big companies are let off the hook when it comes to things like reducing power consumption. The *ball's in our court* for countering global warming and we're not doing enough.

The best of both worlds

Meaning: Getting the benefits of two things at the same time. For example, having children but being able to afford a full-time nanny.

Origin: Probably a reference to the Bible where if a man does good deeds for others while on Earth, he gets to enjoy the rewards in heaven.

Example IELTS question: How do you celebrate birthdays at your workplace?

Possible answer: Well, we have to bring our own cake! I know it seems bad but it's *the best of both worlds*. Nobody has to collect money to buy cakes and then you get a kind that you like on your birthday.

The bottom line

Meaning: The outcome or thing to base a decision on.

Origin: First seen around 1960 in corporate America. The actual bottom line of a profit-loss statement shows whether or not a company made money.

Example IELTS question: Are there many charities in your country?

Possible answer: Yes, there are lots. But *the bottom line* is that the government has to do more to help people. We are paying a lot in taxes but a lot of it is going to things like the military. Our tax dollars should be put to better use for underprivileged people.

The elephant in the room

Meaning: Something obvious and important that nobody wants to talk about.

Origin: First seen in an 1814 fable by Ivan Krylov, "*The Inquisitive Man.*" It tells the story of a man who goes to a museum and notices all sorts of small things but not the elephant.

Example IELTS question: What jobs are the most important to society?

Possible answer: I think most people would give the usual answer like a doctor or a teacher. But *the elephant in the room* is that society is built on low-paid, migrant workers who do things like work in meatpacking plants or on farms. Without them, we'd have no food to eat!

The last straw

Meaning: The final annoying thing before someone loses their patience. For example, a child has been misbehaving all day but his dad finally yelled at him when he wouldn't stay in his room at bedtime.

Origin: First seen in the late 1700s. Camels were often used to transport goods and as much weight as possible was loaded onto them to get the most value from a trip. A final piece of straw was placed on the camel and caused him to collapse, breaking his back.

Example IELTS question: Why do people change jobs?

Possible answer: Well, some people don't mind the job that they have and then leave for something like a better salary or fewer working hours. However, some people have something bad happen at work and it's *the last straw*. For example, their boss yelling at them one last time.

The straw that broke the camel's back

Meaning: The last thing in a series of bad things before an event occurs — like a breakup, quitting a job, or fight.

Origin: First seen in the late 1700s. Camels were often used to transport goods and as much weight as possible was loaded onto them to get the most value from a trip. A final piece of straw was placed on the camel and caused him to collapse, breaking his back.

Example IELTS question: Do you think that there is enough funding for the arts in your country?

Possible answer: Not at all. Prior to Covid-19, funding was barely adequate but then during the pandemic, the government cut funding to almost nothing. That was *the straw that broke the camel's back* and I'm worried that most artists won't be able to survive.

The writing is on the wall

Meaning: Something that is obvious to everyone.

Origin: Related to the Old Testament story of Daniel in the Bible. A mysterious hand wrote a message on a wall for the King and Daniel was able to interpret it.

Example IELTS question: How has teaching changed in your country in the last few decades?

Possible answer: Teachers' salaries haven't kept up with inflation and it's no longer a well-paying job in my country. Fewer and fewer people are going to teacher's college and *the writing is on the wall*—there is going to be a serious teacher shortage in a few years from now. Hopefully teachers' unions can negotiate better salaries and benefits at that time—they'll have the upper hand.

Thinking outside the box
Meaning: Creative thinking about something.

Origin: Probably comes from the marketing and advertising world that wants to gain attention for products.

Example IELTS question: What can bosses do to help their employees be more productive?

Possible answer: In many industries, one of the most important things a boss can do is to encourage employees to *think outside the box* about problems.

Throw in the towel

Meaning: To quit or give up.

Origin: Comes from boxing, where a boxer throws a towel into the ring to indicate that he's giving up.

Example IELTS question: Describe a test that you had to study really hard for.

Possible answer: I took the bar exam 5 years ago and I've never studied as hard in my life as I did for that one! I wanted to *throw in the towel* several times but I'm happy that I persevered.

Tip of the iceberg

Meaning: A very small part of something much bigger, usually a negative thing or a problem.

Origin: It's well known that icebergs contain most of their mass under the water and that you can only see the smallest portions of them above the water.

Example IELTS question: Do you think the Internet is safe for children to use unsupervised?

Possible answer: Not at all! The cyber crimes that we've seen against children are only the *tip of the iceberg*. There's so much more going on that we have no idea about.

Too much time on your hands

Meaning: Not busy enough.

Origin: First seen in the 1800s but the origin is unknown.

Example IELTS question: What's your normal morning routine?

Possible answer: On the weekdays, I'm always rushing around, getting ready for work. I never have *too much time on my hands* as I have a long commute.

Treading water

Meaning: Barely keeping up with work or school.

Origin: Unknown but is likely related to keeping your head above water so that you don't drown.

Example IELTS question: Are you busy at work most days?

Possible answer: Absolutely. We're barely *treading water* most days. My boss is trying to hire some more people but it's hard to find qualified welders.

Twist my arm

Meaning: Convince someone to do something.
Origin: First seen in the 1900s and refers to using physical force to get something done.
Example IELTS question: Do you like eating out?

Possible answer: I'm pretty frugal so usually not. But, my husband *twists my arm* for things like birthdays or anniversaries and I agree to go!

Under the table

Meaning: Something sketchy or illegal.

Under the table: First seen in the mid-1900s regarding money being passed under a table for a bribe.

Example IELTS question: Is there a lot of corruption in your country?

Possible answer: Lots of things happen *under the table*, that's for sure. For example, people do "handshake" deals to avoid paying taxes all the time.

Under the wrong impression

Meaning: Incorrect thinking.

Origin: Uncertain.

Example IELTS question: Do you have a favourite celebrity?

Possible answer: I like Venus Williams. I was *under the wrong impression* about her and thought she was arrogant. But, she's a very smart lady with a good head on her shoulders.

Up in the air

Meaning: Not decided yet.

Origin: Used since the 1700s and refers to particles or things that float around in the air and haven't settled yet.

Example IELTS question: Do you have a plan for your upcoming vacation time?

Possible answer: It's still *up in the air*. My husband wants to go camping but I want to stay at a beach resort. We'll have to see what happens!

Vanished into thin air

Meaning: Disappeared without a trace.

Origin: Shakespeare used the term, "thin air" and similar phrases in many of his works.

Example IELTS question: Describe a book that you read recently.

Possible answer: I recently read a true story about a young child who went missing, Madeline McCann. She *vanished into thin air* when on vacation with her family in Portugal. She is still missing, 20 years later.

Walking a tightrope

Meaning: To do something that requires extreme care and precision; to navigate a situation that allows for no error.

Origin: Uncertain when it came into use but tightrope walking has been around for centuries.

Example IELTS question: Do you think teachers have a difficult job?

Possible answer: Most definitely. They are *walking a tightrope,* dealing with difficult kids, demanding parents and the requirements of the educational system.

Watch my weight

Meaning: Gaining weight easily and having to be careful about what you eat.

Origin: Uncertain.

Example IELTS question: Do you eat junk food?

Possible answer: Hardly ever. I'm trying to *watch my weight* so generally eat fruits and veggies and healthy stuff like that.

Water under the bridge

Meaning: Something from the past that is better forgotten.

Origin: From the 1900s and probably refers to the fact that water which flows under a bridge will never come back the same way. It goes in only one direction.

Example IELTS question: What do you think of the president or prime minister of your country?

Possible answer: Well, she was involved in a scandal about 20 years ago when she was a city councillor but that's mostly *water under the bridge* now. Most people support her.

When pigs fly

Meaning: Something that is very unlikely to happen.

Origin: A similar idiom can be found in various languages and cultures, including Romania, Germany, Scotland, and the USA. Pigs are animals that are unable to fly.

Example IELTS question: Do you like having a tidy home?

Possible answer: Yes, I love it. But now that I have kids, it's impossible to keep the house clean. My kids will pick up after themselves *when pigs fly*!

Weather the storm

Meaning: Make it through, or survive a difficult situation.

Origin: First seen in the 1600s to describe a ship safely making it through a dangerous storm.

Example IELTS question: Do you find your studies difficult?

Possible answer: I'm in my final year now and am getting ready for exams. It's not easy but I just have to *weather the storm* and it'll be over soon.

When it rains, it pours

Meaning: When more than one bad thing happens at the same time.

Origin: Uncertain but made popular by the rapper 50 Cent when he used it in a song.

Example IELTS question: What makes you unhappy?

Possible answer: I hate being so busy at work, especially when my kids need help with homework. And there are always so many permission slips and other forms to fill out for them. *When it rains, it pours*!

Within our reach

Meaning: Can be obtained without too much difficulty.

Origin: Uncertain.

Example IELTS question: Will homelessness ever be solved in your city?

Possible answer: Vancouver has made some big strides with regards to homelessness and putting an end to it is *within our reach*.

Working my fingers to the bone

Meaning: Working very hard, beyond capacity.

Origin: From the 1800s and refers to working so hard that you rub all the skin off your fingers.

Example IELTS question: Do you have a hobby?

Possible answer: Yes, I love cycling but I don't have much time for it these days! I've been *working my fingers to the bone*, studying for an upcoming test.

Work my way up

Meaning: To start at the bottom and work hard to move higher up in a company.

Origin: Unknown.

Example IELTS question: Why did you choose your job?

Possible answer: I chose my job because the company promotes people from within. I want to *work my way up* into management eventually.

Work yourself to death

Meaning: Working too hard.

Origin: Unknown, but could be related to working beyond normal capacity until you're sick.

Example IELTS question: Do you plan to continue with your job in the future?

Possible answer: I'll probably do it for a few more years as the money is good. But, I don't want to *work myself to death*!

Worse for wear

Meaning: Feeling worn out or tired.

Origin: Seen as early as the 1500s and could be referring to someone drunk or hungover.

Example IELTS question: Do you consider yourself to be healthy?

Possible answer: Mostly, yes. But, I am a bit *worse for wear* with all my old injuries from playing sports.

You can't judge a book by its cover

Meaning: To not judge something or someone based on appearance. For example, a restaurant that's not stylish may have delicious food.

Origin: From a 1944 edition of the *African Journal of American Speech*.

Example IELTS question: What makes a good teacher?

Possible answer: I've learned that *you can't always judge a book by its cover*. Sometimes the teachers that are hard on you are the best ones. You can learn a lot from them.

Before You Go

If you found this book useful, please leave a review wherever you bought it. It will help other English learners like yourself find this resource.

You might also be interested in this book: Advanced English Conversation Dialogues (by Jackie Bolen). You can find it wherever you like to buy books. It has hundreds of helpful English phrases and expressions. Learn to speak more fluently in American English.